Post Hill
PRESS

A POST HILL PRESS BOOK

Go the F**k to Jail: An Adult Coloring Book of the Clinton Scandals
©2016 by Post Hill Press. All Rights Reserved.

ISBN: 978-1-68261-267-5

No part of this book may be reproduced, stored in a retrieval system, or transmitted
by any means without the written permission of the Publisher.

http://posthillpress.com

Vincent Foster died in 1993 from a gunshot (or two?) at a suburban Virginia park. Several investigations have ruled his death a suicide, but at least one investigator resigned in protest because he believed the evidence clearly pointed to murder. Foster had a decades-long working relationship with Hillary Clinton, but some believe they had a romantic relationship as well. Foster served as deputy White House counsel to President Bill Clinton, but he was privy to all things Clinton in a way few others in the administration were. Ultimately, Hillary's history of dishonesty and ethics violations leaves open the door to the possibility that she was involved in murder to silence someone who knew too much.

If you're a Clinton, drug money is just as good as any other money when it comes to political or personal use. Remember Jorge Cabrera? He told the DNC to "say hello to 20,000 of my little friends" in the form of cold, hard, cash dollars. Within weeks of writing a check to the Democratic National Committee in 1995, he was standing next to the First Lady for pictures at a White House holiday event. Turns out Cabrera was a drug trafficker. He was arrested shortly after hobnobbing with Hillary, and the DNC begrudgingly returned his donation.

The name Paula Jones immediately conjures up memories of how Bill Clinton, as Governor of Arkansas, propositioned the government employee in a Little Rock motel room. Her lawsuit and subsequent independent counsel investigation tarnished Bill Clinton's presidency and contributed to his ultimate impeachment. Fast forward twenty years, and Paula Jones is back to share her experience with the Clintons, calling Hillary a "bully" and accusing her of being "two-faced." Suddenly, it becomes all too clear what another Clinton presidency would look like for the American people. Dirty laundry just keeps piling up!

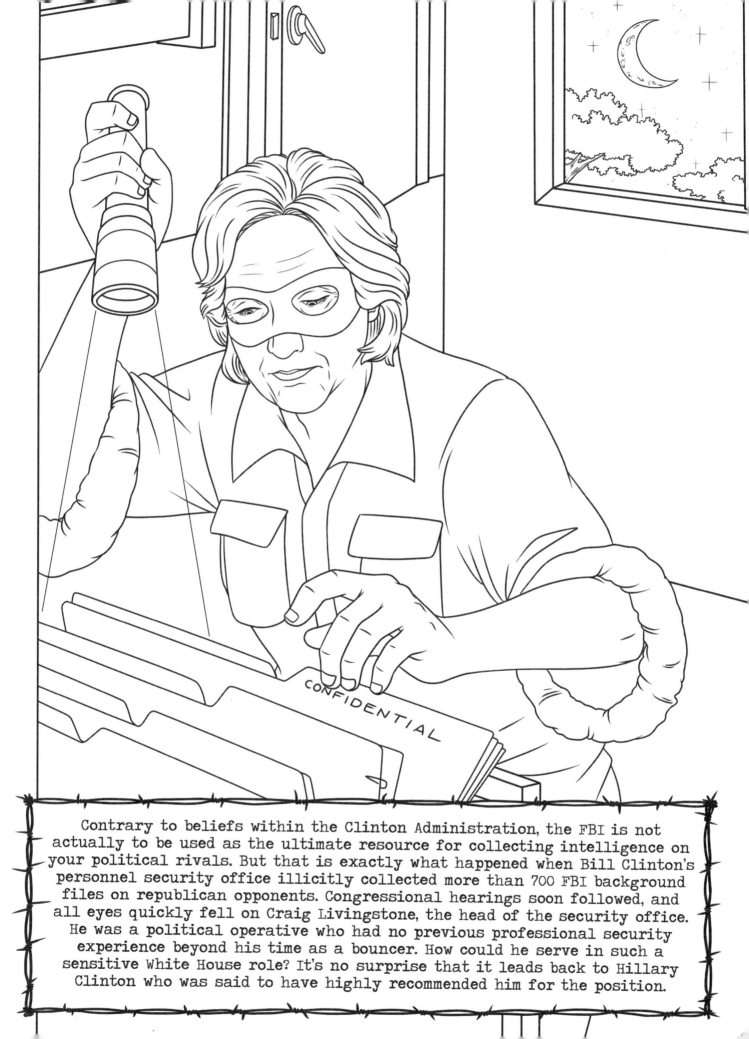

Contrary to beliefs within the Clinton Administration, the FBI is not actually to be used as the ultimate resource for collecting intelligence on your political rivals. But that is exactly what happened when Bill Clinton's personnel security office illicitly collected more than 700 FBI background files on republican opponents. Congressional hearings soon followed, and all eyes quickly fell on Craig Livingstone, the head of the security office. He was a political operative who had no previous professional security experience beyond his time as a bouncer. How could he serve in such a sensitive White House role? It's no surprise that it leads back to Hillary Clinton who was said to have highly recommended him for the position.

VAST RIGHT-WING CONSPIRACY

Bill Clinton is a habitual user of women to fulfill his sexual desires, and Hillary Clinton is his biggest defender. From Paula Jones to Gennifer Flowers, Kathleen Willey and Monica Lewinsky (among many others), Hillary went before the nation time and again to discredit and defame the very women who had already been victimized by her husband. In the case of Monica Lewinsky, Hillary went on a national morning show and said the allegations were nothing more than a "vast, right-wing conspiracy." Of course, that was before the world found out about the infamous stain on that blue dress.

Who makes the best political fundraisers? Fugitives, of course! Norman Hsu was such a man who used his criminal inclinations to raise hundreds of thousands of dollars for the Democratic Party and prominent candidates. During Hillary's 2008 presidential campaign, Hsu collected some $850,000. The only problem was, she had to return all of it when Hsu was discovered to be a fugitive on the run from fraud charges. He tried to explain that he was in good company of fellow fraudsters with the Clinton campaign, but he now sits in a federal penitentiary, serving a 292-month sentence.

That silly Hillary got our hopes up yet again only to leave us in utter disappointment. During her 2008 presidential bid, she recounted a story of landing in Bosnia "under sniper fire." Most of America gleefully imagined Hillary crouching beneath windows and ducking under chairs as bullets whizzed by just out of reach. But it was all a big lie. When pressed for corroboration of her claim, she said she "made a mistake" in retelling the event. Perhaps Hillary and Brian Williams could one-up one another by sharing their tall tales of danger and despair!

AIRPLANE TICKET ✈

Passenger : HILLARY CLINTON

Destination : PRISON

Departure : IMMEDIATELY

This travel itinerary courtesy of the White House Travel Office

CHANCE — GO DIRECTLY TO JAIL

DO NOT PASS
DO NOT COLLECT $ 200

Hillary Clinton gets what Hillary Clinton wants, ethics or right versus wrong be damned. This proved true yet again as Hillary assumed the role of First Lady of the United States. Hillary wanted all the members of the White House Travel Office terminated and replaced with a travel agency she worked with during the presidential campaign. For fear of unleashing Hillary's wrath, the employees were fired in one fell swoop; the Travelgate scandal was born - and America is still trying to find a way to book Hillary a one way ticket to some far off, not-so-tropical destination.

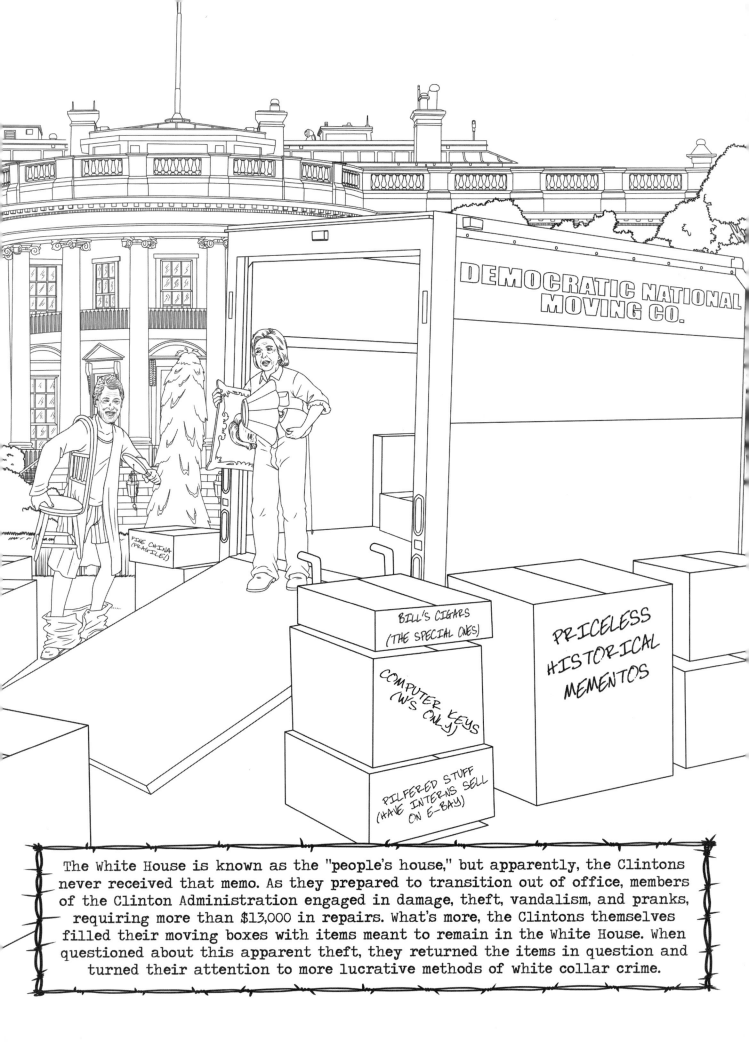

The White House is known as the "people's house," but apparently, the Clintons never received that memo. As they prepared to transition out of office, members of the Clinton Administration engaged in damage, theft, vandalism, and pranks, requiring more than $13,000 in repairs. What's more, the Clintons themselves filled their moving boxes with items meant to remain in the White House. When questioned about this apparent theft, they returned the items in question and turned their attention to more lucrative methods of white collar crime.

What do you do when you're the governor of a state where Tyson Foods Inc. has a huge interest in friendly government oversight? You have your wife cozy up with the top legal advisor of that company of course, and then you reap the financial rewards when that company officially makes investment decisions on your behalf. This occurred in the realm of cattle futures trading, where she earned close to $100,000 in the late 1970s. Hillary had no idea how to trade cattle futures, but Tyson knew how to bribe the governor, and she felt right at home amongst all the manure.

Politicians deliver speeches for a living, but apparently those speeches can be worth hundreds of thousands of dollars when you deliver them as a private individual, and your last name is Clinton. Hillary reported earnings of more than $11 million in speaking fees over a thirteen month period. Many people question whether these payments were for her incredible wisdom or if they were merely down payments on future favors should she con her way into the most powerful office in the world. The latter is hard to deny. It's quite possible that Hillary's speeches could hold the record for being the most expensive hot air ever sold.

Whitewater is the first major scandal associated with the Clintons, but it highlights how Bill and Hillary view the power of public office as a mechanism to enrich themselves and their friends., and have done so dating back to the 1970s. More than a difficult to decipher land deal with a shady loan thrown into the mix, the scandal is one of the earliest indications that the Clinton family will do or say whatever it takes to promote their self-interests and then feign shock when their schemes are discovered. It's the exact same formula for "success" that Hillary uses to this very day.

As Secretary of State, Hillary Clinton was responsible for coordinating and implementing the foreign policy of the United States. What she actually did was leverage her position to further the interests of the wealthiest individuals and businesses, both at home and abroad. In exchange for her unscrupulous acts, the Clinton Foundation, the Hillary presidential campaign, and the Clinton family itself accepted tens of millions of dollars in financial contributions and other monetary payments. Conflicts of interest were refuted, denied, disclaimed, and ignored. Meanwhile, it would be challenging to find examples of the Secretary going out of her way for those who couldn't offer big checks in return.

As Secretary of State, Hillary Clinton viewed her role as saleswoman in chief for some of America's largest corporations. Instead of raising human rights and free speech concerns while in Russia, she used her time to deliver a "shameless pitch" for Boeing, the largest aerospace company in the world. The pitch worked. Boeing signed a multi-billion-dollar deal with a Russian airline. Right afterward, Boeing, coincidentally, gave generously to the Clinton Foundation and Bill Clinton himself, a fat sum totaling more than a million dollars. Could it be that Hillary used her governmental power and influence to make sure the Clintons continue flying high?

Nearly twenty percent of the energy used in the USA is produced by nuclear power, uranium being a key component. Enter Russia, who sought to assume a 51 percent controlling interest in a company that owns most of the world's uranium deposits, including one fifth of the production capacity of the United States. When a foreign government seeks to buy such a strategic asset, our government has safeguards in place to protect its interests. One layer of such safeguards was supposed to be Secretary of State Hillary Clinton. Is it any surprise that Hillary enthusiastically gave Putin the green light? Coincidentally, the Clinton Foundation received nearly $3 million in payments from key stakeholders in the transaction. Now Putin has his finger on our nation's light switch and could say "lights out" at any time,

Under Hillary Clinton's "leadership" as Secretary of State, U.S. Ambassador Chris Stevens and three other Americans were brutally murdered during a terrorist attack in Benghazi, Libya. Requests for additional security were ignored. Clinton's attempt to shift blame on an obscure Internet video was nothing more than a political red herring. A House committee investigative report held no smoking gun, but her ineptitude in dealing with a highly caustic situation is easily seen in the 800-page report. After the report's release, Hillary told the media, "I think it's pretty clear it's time to move on." Tell that to the families who lost their loved ones, Hillary. And keep telling that to yourself while you try to sleep with a clear conscience.

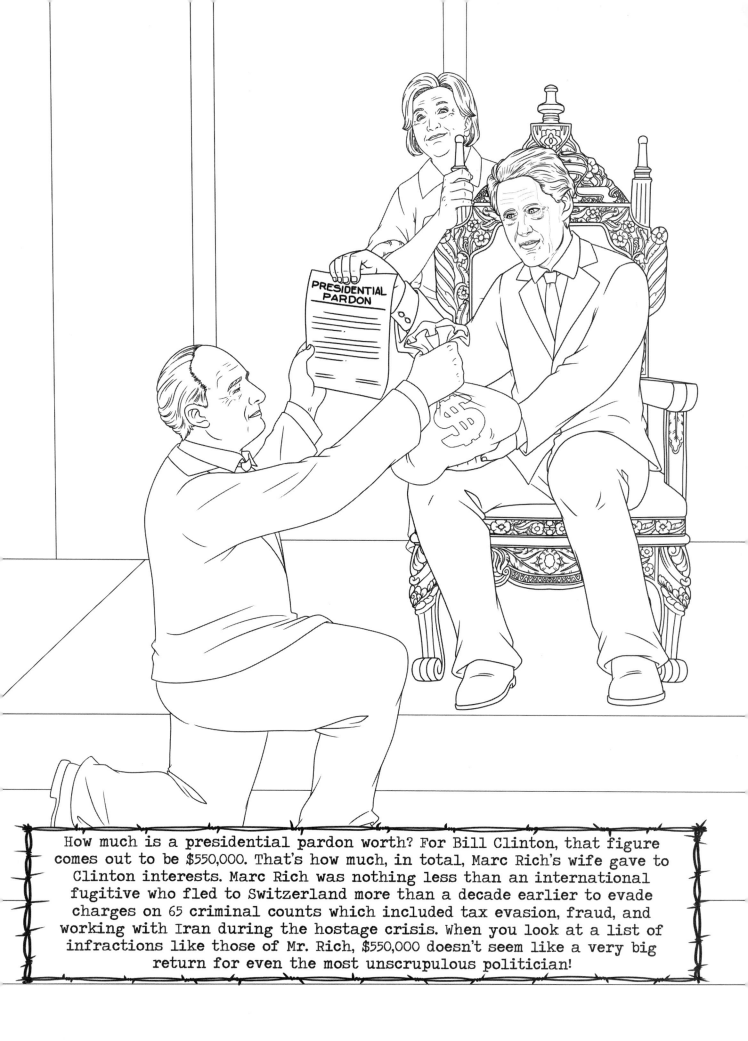

How much is a presidential pardon worth? For Bill Clinton, that figure comes out to be $550,000. That's how much, in total, Marc Rich's wife gave to Clinton interests. Marc Rich was nothing less than an international fugitive who fled to Switzerland more than a decade earlier to evade charges on 65 criminal counts which included tax evasion, fraud, and working with Iran during the hostage crisis. When you look at a list of infractions like those of Mr. Rich, $550,000 doesn't seem like a very big return for even the most unscrupulous politician!

Whether you're a peon intern at the State Department or the Secretary of State, you're still a government employee, and government employees use email addresses that run on government computers - unless you're Hillary Clinton. If you're Hillary Clinton, then you set up a computer in your own home and have all of your highly sensitive, classified work email transferred through that computer. Because, if nothing else, doing so is an example of astute judgment, right? No! Actually, it shows how Hillary wouldn't pass as a customer service agent at a cable or satellite TV company, let alone the upper echelons of the United States government!

For youngsters, "Which of These is Not Like the Others" is a fun game to play with friends. For politically-minded adults, it's also a way to identify some of Hillary Clinton's top financial backers. Rajiv Fernando was one such Clinton devotee, who donated heavily to Hillary's '08 presidential bid and to the Clinton Foundation. Fast forward to Secretary Clinton running the State Department, and Fernando is placed on a high-level intelligence advisory board among some of the top experts in the country. His qualifications? He was a successful securities trader who was "good with technology." Is it a coincidence that he also poured cash into the Clinton coffers? This game is a lot more fun when our national security isn't involved.

You've probably never seen Harold Geisel, but if you would like to picture him in your mind, then simply imagine a puppet-man who is exactly the size of Hillary Clinton's hand. In 2013, Geisel served as Interim Inspector General for the State Department, a position that, apparently, has authority in name only. The job of an Inspector General is to inspect an organization or agency independently, in this case, the State Department. However, the *Washington Examiner* newspaper uncovered that his work was not at all independent. When comparing an early draft of his work with final publications, damaging information was removed to protect Hillary and her State Department cohorts. The secretive reach of the Secretary of State had no limits.

When you connect the crossed paths of Hillary Clinton, Gilbert Chagoury, and Boko Haram, you discover an elaborate web of lies and deceit that potentially influence U.S. terrorism policy. Chagoury is the founder of one of Nigeria's biggest construction companies, and he's had a history of financially supporting Bill Clinton's campaign and philanthropic endeavors for over two decades. His support totals in the tens of millions of dollars. Now, enter Secretary of State Clinton, who found herself in the position of having to determine whether Boko Haram, the Nigerian terrorist group, should be labeled as a Foreign Terrorist Organization. As you might imagine, Chagoury's Nigerian construction efforts would plummet in value if Boko Haram received such a designation. No surprise ending here. It appears as though Hillary protected her friend at the expense of national security.

Sex scandals seem to follow Hillary no matter where she goes, and her response is always the same: refute and cover up. Most recently, the Clinton State Department impeded the official investigation into State Department employees soliciting prostitutes while overseas on official business. Numerous officials reported that their efforts to uncover the true details of the hazardous behavior were met with political interference and restrictions on access to vital documents. Ultimately, three of the employees who exhibited the most egregious behavior received suspensions of just a single day. Perhaps this punitive action falls in line with Hillary's equally toothless personal approach of forcing Bill to sleep on the couch each time she uncovers one of his numerous sexual indiscretions.

Iranian ambitions to create a nuclear weapon capable of destabilizing the global economy and literally destroying our closest allies, conjured up a "robust" policy of sanctions - sanctions with exceptions. The sanctions were to forbid companies from doing business with Iran, and the exceptions, of course, were simply exempting those players who curried great favor for the Secretary of State and her personal interests. In this particular case of scandalous behavior, the Swedes bent over backwards to support the Clinton Foundation, laying down roots in its country. As an apparent extension of gratitude, Clinton's State Department excluded every Swedish company from its sanctions list. It seems that even the threat of nuclear proliferation can be overlooked if some personal gain to the Clintons can be attained.

Pop quiz: Who enjoys the mineral rights to the most valuable natural resources in the Congo? Is it the Congolese government, or a company based in Canada? If your answer is the Canadian company, with the support of Hillary Clinton and her State Department, then you're an excellent student of the corruption of Clinton politics. In this instance, two of the biggest players in the mineral industry made more than $100 million in donations to the Clinton Foundation. As Secretary of State, Hillary intervened to shut out the Congolese government from its own resources, and the world saw once again that the most valuable resource of all is the influence of Hillary Clinton, which is perpetually for sale to the highest bidder.

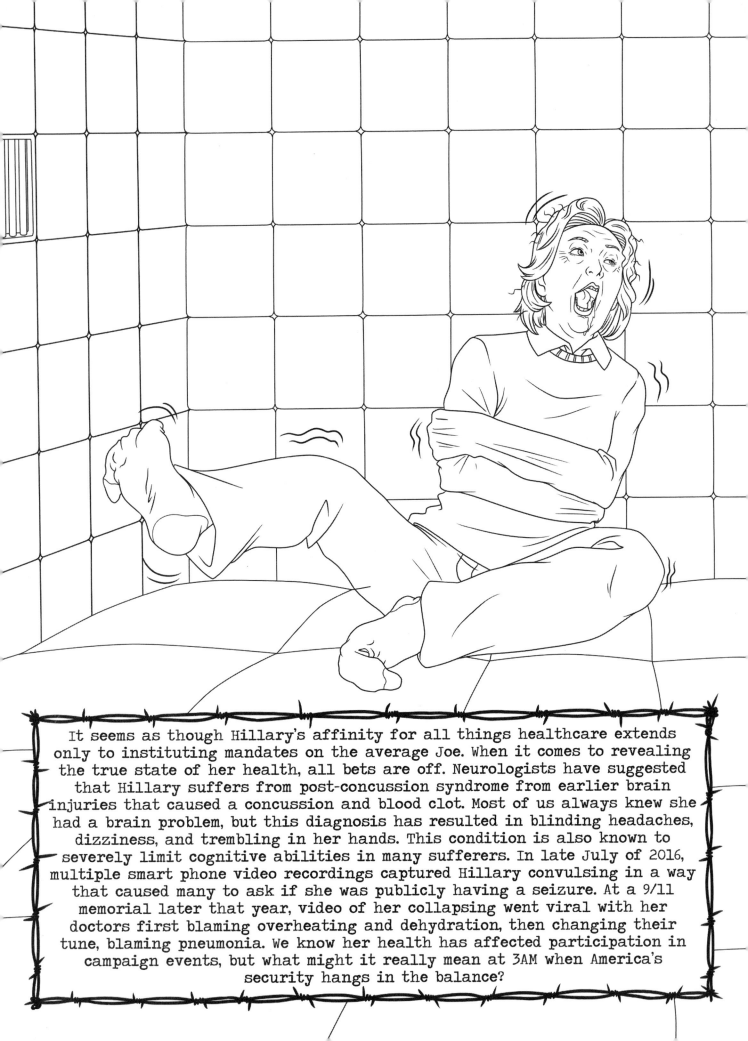

It seems as though Hillary's affinity for all things healthcare extends only to instituting mandates on the average Joe. When it comes to revealing the true state of her health, all bets are off. Neurologists have suggested that Hillary suffers from post-concussion syndrome from earlier brain injuries that caused a concussion and blood clot. Most of us always knew she had a brain problem, but this diagnosis has resulted in blinding headaches, dizziness, and trembling in her hands. This condition is also known to severely limit cognitive abilities in many sufferers. In late July of 2016, multiple smart phone video recordings captured Hillary convulsing in a way that caused many to ask if she was publicly having a seizure. At a 9/11 memorial later that year, video of her collapsing went viral with her doctors first blaming overheating and dehydration, then changing their tune, blaming pneumonia. We know her health has affected participation in campaign events, but what might it really mean at 3AM when America's security hangs in the balance?

Want to receive an education in how to use power and influence to garner big financial gains for you and your family? Well, look no further than Hillary's unrepentant use of her position as Secretary of State to reward Douglas Becker with tens of millions of dollars in State Department grants for his education initiative. Who is Douglas Becker? He just happens to be the CEO of Laureate Education, a for-profit college that operates in some of the most impoverished regions of the world. And by the way, Becker also named Bill Clinton "Honorary Chancellor" of Laureate Education, a position that resulted in a payout of more than $16 million for the Clintons. It's a new type of mathematics, where greed and corruption are always the bottom line.

A recent survey showed that slippery politicians and slimy lawyers who defend child rapists have an equal likelihood of going to Hell. Hillary has doubled her chances, since she's both! At just 27-years old and as a member of the State Bar of Arkansas, Hillary's path crossed that of a factory worker accused of raping a twelve-year-old girl. Like a greyhound who loves the scent of injustice, Hillary sniffed out every technical evidentiary mishap, and was victorious in reducing the charge from first-degree rape to a plea of unlawful fondling of a minor under the age of 14. With this, the bright young attorney embarked on her journey of empowering women everywhere!

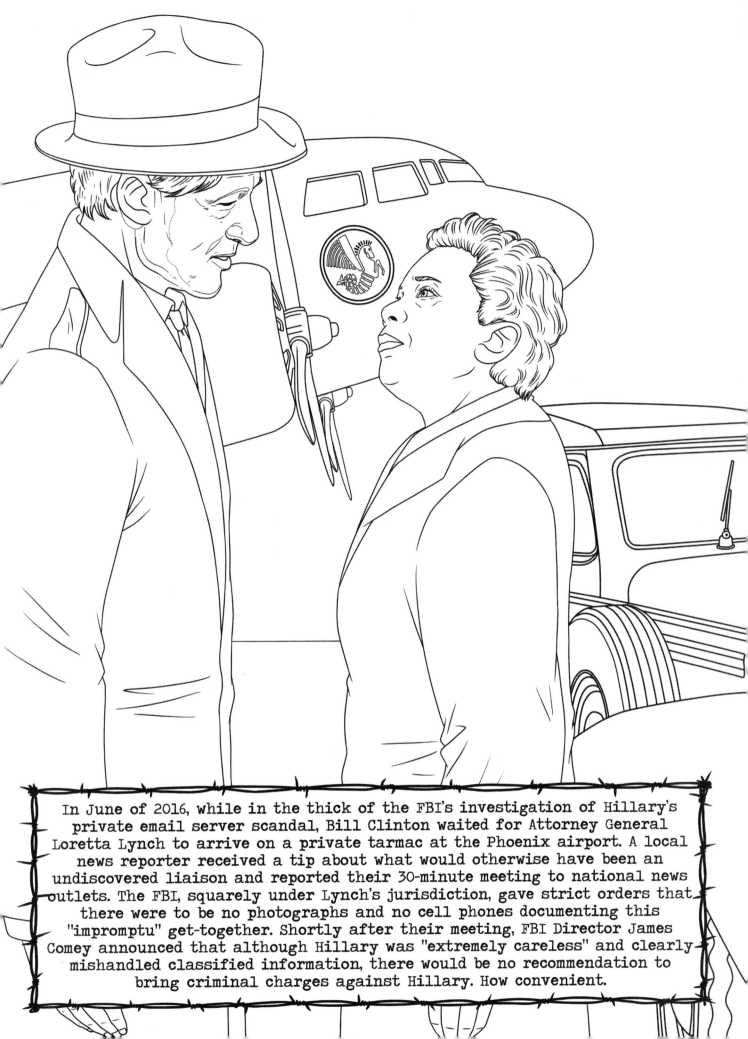

In June of 2016, while in the thick of the FBI's investigation of Hillary's private email server scandal, Bill Clinton waited for Attorney General Loretta Lynch to arrive on a private tarmac at the Phoenix airport. A local news reporter received a tip about what would otherwise have been an undiscovered liaison and reported their 30-minute meeting to national news outlets. The FBI, squarely under Lynch's jurisdiction, gave strict orders that there were to be no photographs and no cell phones documenting this "impromptu" get-together. Shortly after their meeting, FBI Director James Comey announced that although Hillary was "extremely careless" and clearly mishandled classified information, there would be no recommendation to bring criminal charges against Hillary. How convenient.

Days before the 2016 Democratic National Primary, Wikileaks released thousands of email messages obtained by Russian hackers from the Democratic National Committee's email servers. These messages contained damning evidence pointing to the DNC fixing the nomination in Hillary's favor by working to sabotage the campaign of her opponent, Bernie Sanders. Shortly following the public data dump, DNC chairwoman, Debbie Wasserman Schultz, announced she would resign. Mere hours following her resignation, Hillary issued a statement proclaiming her gratefulness to Wasserman Schultz's "leadership" and went on to announce that the disgraced Wasserman Schultz would take a prominent role in the Clinton campaign as an honorary chair. It seems as though birds of a feather campaign together.

As this book began taking shape, it was no challenge finding situations ripe with the fingerprints of Hill and Bill. In the weeks of research that followed, this book seemed to write itself. Like clockwork, new scandals arose in the press in which Hillary or her cohorts became convenient beneficiaries. Where there's smoke, there's fire. Because of the seemingly unending string of new damning evidence implicating the Clintons' and their cronies' shady tactics, it became necessary to add this blank page for you to insert your own drawings here so that this volume can be kept up to date. The lies and deception beg the question, isn't it time they "Go the F ∗ ∗ k to Jail"?